WILD LIVES

D0601514

SWIMMING WITH
SHARKS

NICK ARNOLD

ILLUSTRATED BY JANE COPE

■SCHOLASTIC

To Mum – thanks for my teeth, my feet and
everything else

Scholastic Children's Books,
Commonwealth House, 1–19 New Oxford Street,
London WC1A 1NU, UK

A division of Scholastic Ltd
London – New York – Toronto – Sydney – Auckland
Mexico City – New Delhi – Hong Kong

Copyright © Nick Arnold, 2003
Illustrations copyright © Jane Cope, 2003

ISBN 0 439 99425 X

Printed and bound in Great Britain
by Cox & Wyman Ltd, Reading, Berkshire
Cover shark image supplied by the Bruce Coleman Collection

2 4 6 8 10 9 7 5 3 1

The right of Nick Arnold and Jane Cope to be identified as the
author and illustrator of this work has been asserted by them in accordance with the
Copyright, Designs and Patents Act, 1988.

CONTENTS

 **CALLING ALL TEACHERS!**

DARE YOU TAKE THE PLUNGE?

If you're sick of school – and you're NOT scared of sharks, Wildwatch wants to hear from you! We're after a teacher (with scuba diving experience) to swim with killer sharks! Your job will be to watch a great white shark and keep a diary.

❑ *See great white sharks really close up*
❑ *Enjoy the ULTIMATE diving experience*
❑ *Action, adventure and drama guaranteed!*

❑ *Excellent pay, plus expenses, including travel to Australia*
❑ *Your diary will be published by Wildwatch!*

DON'T DELAY – APPLY TODAY...

The shark was coming for me...

I stared in horror and its cruel black eyes stared back. Its bullet-shaped nose pointed straight at me and its snarling mouth opened greedily. The shark was hungry, as hungry as the empty-bellied ocean

that swallows everything and still comes back for a second helping.

The shark zoomed through the water. Closer and closer it came. Its huge jaws opened wider and wider. I screamed, but nothing came out except bubbles. Then the shark bit me. I felt nothing – the pain was beyond feeling. My whole world blew apart into blood and messy fleshy bits. I beat my arms, I struggled feebly and then … I woke up!

I rubbed my eyes sleepily and wondered whether answering the advert had been some kind of mistake. I'm an English teacher, my name is Sebastian Walters (but *please* call me Seb) and I've just got the Wildwatch job.

In six weeks' time I'll be swimming with sharks. I must be crazy…

This is my diary.

THIS IS ME

SCARY SHARKS AND TIMID TEACHERS

March 1

Let's go back to the day I saw the advert…

I looked in the mirror and saw a skinny, pale-faced teacher. But inside a battle was raging.

"*Go on!* Apply for the job," urged my secret adventurous self. "You've always dreamt of swimming with sharks."

"What about the danger?" worried my more timid side.

"Prove you're brave enough!" dared brave Seb.

"But what about my house, my job…?" wailed timid Seb.

TIMID SEB

"Your life is boring and you're sick of school," sneered brave Seb.

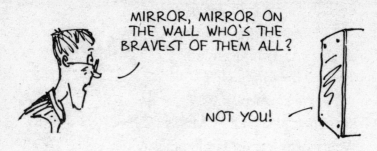

That evening I thought more about the advert, but I couldn't make up my mind. So I made myself a mug of hot chocolate and watched TV until it was time to go to bed. I knew something was missing from my life, but I wasn't sure about the Wildwatch job – did I *really* have the courage to swim with sharks?

March 2

During the morning break I was chatting to Mrs Wentworth – she's the other English teacher. "I've seen a job," I remarked. "It's only for four months but it's in Australia."

"Australia!" exclaimed Mrs Wentworth. "Oooh how lovely. All that sun and scenery!"

"The job involves swimming with great white sharks," I said.

The busy staffroom fell silent. Everyone was staring at me. It was as if I'd announced that I was going to empty a large potty over the head teacher's head.

Eyes widened, jaws dropped and old Mr Turner the art teacher spat a mouthful of tea over his trousers.

"I expect it'll be most ... *interesting*," said Mrs Wentworth in a faint faraway voice. She gave me the sort of look normally reserved for bungee jumpers and crocodile wrestlers.

"Sharks! That's a joke!" snorted Mr Masham the PE teacher. "Seb ain't brave enough to watch sharks on TV! Hey, is this for me?" He plonked himself down on my chair, took a noisy slurp of my coffee and helped himself to my sticky bun.

"Th-th-that's where you're wr-wrong actually!" I stammered.

"Yeah right!" sneered Mr Masham with his mouth full of sticky bun.

"Is this your wall stapler, Seb?" demanded Miss Swift the drama teacher, waving it under my nose. "I'll bring it back later!" she yelled, dashing out.

"Where are my pens and videos you borrowed last term?" I wanted to call after her.

"Go on, apply for the job!" jeered Mr Masham. "I dare you!" He took another bite of my sticky bun and stuck his feet on my newspaper.

Something snapped quietly inside me. I was sick of the way the other teachers treated me.

"I'm going to," I said, bunching my fists. "Actually, that's just what I was going to do today – just you see if I don't!"

And I sent off the coupon as soon as I got home.

March 15

"You know great white sharks are extremely dangerous? If you go it'll be at your own risk," said the nice lady who interviewed me at Wildwatch.

I nodded.

She asked if the danger worried me.

"N-n-no," I said, trying not to stammer. My cup of tea rattled in its saucer.

"Well, I'm sure you'll be OK," she said with a reassuring smile. "You'll be with a group of Australian scientists who are making a study of great whites off Dangerous Reef in South Australia. They're experts and I'm sure they'll look after you. And they do have a safety cage for you to dive in."

I asked what my job would be.

"You won't actually be part of the scientific team, but we're asking you to sail with them and write your diary about one of the sharks they find."

Dangerous Reef. My adventurous self pictured me

crossing swords with pirates, beating off man-eating sharks and digging up buried treasure.

"It sounds really exciting!" I said with enthusiasm.

"Oh, I'm so glad you're interested," said the lady brightly. "We're looking for a keen person! If you're successful, we'll get back to you in a couple of days."

When I got home I started going through the interview in my head. Then I thought back to how I first became interested in sharks. My dad is a marine biologist, and I reckon that it was hearing him talk about sharks that got me going.

I dug out my old shark books, I've still got quite a few, and I found this old photo. Yes, I even played with a plastic shark in the bath!

ME AGED ≤IX

March 18

Wildwatch didn't tell me why I got the job. I suppose I was the most suitable person they interviewed. Well I *am* a teacher *and* I've got diving experience *and* I'm interested in sharks – which is just what they were after. Anyway, now I've got the job, I really ought to jot down a few basic notes...

SEB'S SHARK NOTES
SHARK BASICS

1. A shark is a type of fish. But unlike ordinary fish, shark skeletons are made of a rubbery substance called cartilage. Prod your nose or ear – they're cartilage, too. Cartilage gives a shark a bendy lightweight body.

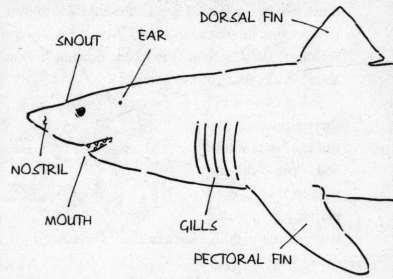

SNOUT

EAR

DORSAL FIN

NOSTRIL

MOUTH

GILLS

PECTORAL FIN

2. Sharks breathe oxygen dissolved in the water that wafts over their gills. Certain sharks, like the great white, have to swim all the time to keep the water moving. When they stop they can't breathe, and if they stop too long they die.

3. Sharks can be very big, or fairly small. Many sharks are shorter than a man's arm and most of them grow less than three metres long.

4. Sharks have large oily livers. Since oil is lighter than water, the liver helps to stop the shark from sinking.

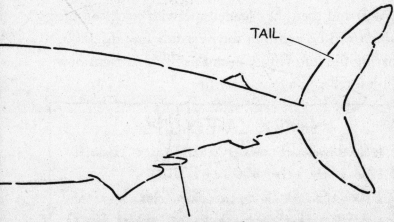

TAIL

MALE SHARKS HAVE TWO CLASPERS
FOR USE IN MATING

5. Shark skin feels rough because it's made of teeth! The close-packed tiny gnashers are known as denticles.

6. Of the 400 or so different types of shark, the largest, fiercest and hungriest shark that attacks people is the great white.

So am I scared of them?

Um, can you keep a secret? The answer's definitely … *yes!*

March 25

Yesterday I went on a training day at Wildwatch. I had to have a medical to check I was fit to dive (I was) and then they loaded me with stacks of info which will be useful in the next few months. I'll be sharing the info with you in this diary, so right now I'll just tell you a few safety tips:

SHARK SAFETY TIPS

1. Never swim with cuts or grazes. Sharks can sniff blood in the water 400 metres away.

2. Don't go for a dip at dawn, dusk or after nightfall - that's when sharks are looking for a bite to eat.

3. Never pee in the sea - sharks don't mind you using their living space as a toilet, but they could home in on the smell.

4. Never swim alone - great white sharks snap up seals on their own and they may hunt lone humans.

5. Don't splash - sharks can mistake your hands and feet for flapping injured fish and they may accidentally bite them off.

6. Never swim when there are lots of fishermen around - sharks like nothing better than a flapping injured fish.

7. Don't wear metal or jewellery - sharks sense the electrical currents that metal gives off in salt water, and the gleam of metal looks like shiny fish scales.

8. Bright yellow, the colour of life jackets, is known as "yum-yum yellow" to shark experts. Sharks love it for some reason, so don't dare wear it!

SPOT THE DIFFERENCE

9. Don't wear different colours - sharks might mistake you for a stripy fish.

10. If you see a shark, get out of the water. But do it slowly! If the shark spots movement it might decide to bite you.

At this point my Wildwatch instructor, an experienced diver named Steve, shrugged cheerfully and said, "Of course if you want to see a great white in the water you'll have to ignore most of this advice, just don't break too many rules in one go."

"But what about the metal?" I asked. "Surely my diving tank is made of metal?"

"Yes, good point," agreed Steve. "That's a risk all divers have to take!"

I went home with my brain popping like popcorn on a hotplate. Swimming with sharks sounds very dangerous and I'm not exactly the lion-tamer sort. I'm not even sure I'd make it as a *kitten* tamer. But I still wanted to prove myself and I love the thought of diving in a new part of the world.

WHOAAAH!

MEOW!

It's hard to explain why I like diving so much. I'm as sporty as a sack of potatoes. But I've loved the water ever since my first yell and splash, or at least that's what my dad says. I've been scuba diving since I was a teenager and I've never looked back! But I've never dived with sharks before. And I'm still having nightmares. Last night I dreamt I was chased around a rock by a giant shark in a pirate's hat.

BLOOD, BOATS AND FISH SLIME

April 8

Welcome to Australia! Yes, I'm here in Oz. My flight was hassle-free, just very L–O–N–G. It felt longer than a flight to Pluto and it was much less interesting! I spent my time reading shark books and watching boring movies.

On the way from Adelaide airport my taxi driver found out why I was here. He shook his head in disbelief. "Don't be a blathering idiot!" he said. "Sharks are vicious. You might as well dive with a ticking bomb!"

I stammered something about being careful.

"It's not a matter of being careful!" growled the driver as he swerved into the path of a truck. "If sharks were people, Mr Shark would be a mean kinda fella. He doesn't have mates, he's only got hangers-on and people he ain't eaten yet!"

Then he told me the latest attack story by "white pointers" or "white death" as they call them around here.

YER BETTA WATCH OUT!

"Terrible business. Woman on holiday – diving for scallops – no chance. Don't suppose she knew what hit her!"

"Did they find her body?" I asked nervously.

"Only her arm."

I took a deep breath, and said nothing as I wondered about safer jobs. Maybe I could be an assistant to a short-sighted knife-thrower?

I'm now at a hotel in Adelaide and I'm very, very worn out. It must be jet lag kicking in. I think I'll crash out. Night, night, readers!

April 10

Yesterday I parked my backside on a coach to Port Lincoln, South Australia, home for great-white watchers. And that's how I came to be at the Balmoral Hotel being fussed over by Mrs Mallory.

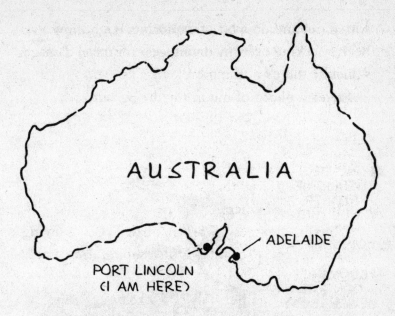

AUSTRALIA

ADELAIDE

PORT LINCOLN
(I AM HERE)

And am I enjoying it! For one thing, Mrs Mallory is serious about breakfast. She cuts toast thick, and serves eggs yolky with factory-sized portions of sizzling bacon. Mrs Mallory says, "Seb, you need filling up and filling out – you look like a stick insect on a diet." The scientists are in 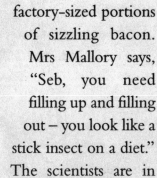 Port Adelaide loading up their ship and the plan is that I'll meet them here the day after tomorrow. So that gives me some time to get over my jet lag, get sorted out and do a bit of exploring. Right now I've been checking over my diving gear for travel damage – luckily there's nothing broken!

Here's a photo of me in my diving suit:

❶ ONE-PIECE NEOPRENE RUBBER WET SUIT

❷ DIVING MASK

❸ BUOYANCY CONTROL DEVICE (BCD)

❹ WEIGHT BELT

❺ AIR TANK

❻ REGULATOR

SEB'S SHARK NOTES
MY DIVING KIT

1. The *wet suit* is a suit that lets water in! The water's cold enough to make a penguin go "BRRRRR!" – but my body warms the water until it's like a radiator. The suit (plus boots and gloves) protects my skin against scratches.

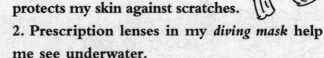

2. Prescription lenses in my *diving mask* help me see underwater.

3. The *BCD* works like a life jacket. I let air escape from the valve to sink and add air from my tank to float at the surface.

4. The *weight belt* helps me sink.

5. The *air tank* is packed with air under pressure.

6. The *regulator* contains a valve that lets me breathe air from my tank at the same pressure as the surrounding sea.

April 11

This morning was bright and sunny. I got up extra early and set off up the hill above Port Lincoln to admire the view. From up there I could see the blue Boston Bay spread out in front of me. Even big yachts looked like expensive toy models and I could make out the hazy humps of islands in the distance.

Here's a map of the area:

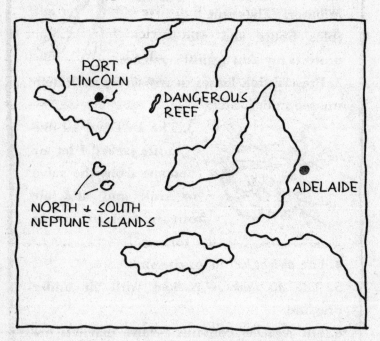

Just then a nasty thought popped up from the murky depths of my brain – somewhere out there in the deep, blue, foam-flecked yonder lurked huge hungry fish. And soon I would be meeting them face to face! Despite the sunshine, I felt cold and shivery and all the little hairs on my arms stood up.

SEB'S SHARK NOTES
PLACES TO FIND GREAT WHITES

1. Great whites like water that's cool but not too cold.
2. Great whites lurk around rocky islands where seals and sea lions live – like Dyer and Seal Islands in South Africa, the Farallon Islands off California, and the Neptune Islands and Dangerous Reef off South Australia.

EEK!

April 12

I've just had a call from the scientists. They're still in Port Adelaide because of some kind of computer glitch in ordering stores. So I'm marooned in Port Lincoln for the rest of the week (yawn, sigh).

April 15

Port Lincoln has a busy harbour where trawlers tie up and fishy smells linger. I've strolled down the bustling streets named after British cities; I've shopped in the shopping mall; mooched by the marina; lounged in the leisure centre and jogged on the jetty – and I reckon I've done everything.

To be honest I'm a bit put out. I've been in Port Lincoln nearly a week and I haven't been anywhere near a shark. Oh well, I suppose I'll just have to be patient!

April 17

The scientists are finally here! Hooray – NO MORE WAITING! This evening I met them for supper at a local restaurant. As usual with new people I felt a bit awkward, but I found out the basics:

Name: Professor Gerald Winterton
Age: 50
Job: The galaxy's leading shark expert

The Professor went on for ten hours (that's how it felt to

me) about all the expeditions he's led in 25 years of research. Before the meal, he was helping himself from a bag of jelly babies. But he didn't offer me one.

Name: Andy Hawkins
Age: 45
Job: Captain of our ship

Andy's a weather-beaten ex-diver. He hires his ship out for cruises and science trips and he's really into great whites. In fact he dreams of swimming with one *without* a safety cage!!!! Apart from that he seems fairly normal in a quiet, laid-back sort of way.

Name: Nathan Forest
Age: 23
Job: Studies shark behaviour

Nathan is the dippiest scientist I've ever met. He says sharks aren't dangerous, they're just "sort of misunderstood" and he enjoys feeding bull sharks by hand. He's still got all his fingers, though – I counted them just to make sure!

Name: Katie Summers
Age: 24
Job: Studies reef
shark senses

Katie shuddered when Nathan talked about bull sharks and said that they sounded "awful dangerous", but she thinks reef sharks are "real sweeties" and she likes to *cuddle* them. She'd like to *kiss* a great white – but wonders if it's "a teeny bit risky".

Nathan and Katie were students at the Professor's university and they've taken time off from their own shark projects to help on this trip. Having finished his lecture on previous trips, the Professor explained what they were planning to do (complete with long scientific words).

Fishermen have been seeing fewer and fewer great whites around Dangerous Reef and the Neptune Islands and the scientists want to build up a picture of the sharks still living in the area. They want to study as many sharks as possible and find out whether they're old or young, male or female. They also want to check if sharks stay in one place or whether they move around, by placing a sound tracker on a shark and following it.

The Professor quizzed me about my knowledge of sharks and whether I had funeral and hospital insurance.

"This is no pleasure cruise," he said, giving me a stern stare over the top of his glasses. "Great whites are highly dangerous. We'll have a cage, of course, but the metal bars produce electrical currents that actually attract sharks and some sharks are strong enough to break the bars and take a diver. It's never been known, but…"

I quickly assured him that I knew about the dangers and that Wildwatch had arranged the insurance.

I don't think Gerald's too happy I'm coming. Returning from the toilet, I heard his booming voice complaining, "…ONLY A TEACHER … NOT EVEN A SCIENTIST … HE'LL USE UP VALUABLE DIVING TIME!"

I hid in the toilet for 20 minutes so I wouldn't walk in on an awkward scene.

April 18

Andy must have settled things with Gerald because he was perfectly polite when we all met up this morning. I'd come to the quay to look over Andy's ship, the *Natalie*, and help load a few stores.

❶ SHARK CAGE TO PROTECT DIVERS

❷ UPPER DECK

❸ LIFTING ARM

❹ RADIO AERIAL

❺ STERN

❻ BOW

❼ DIVING PLATFORM

❽ MAIN CABIN AND GALLEY

Below deck are three tiny cabins each with a set of bunks. There's an equally microscopic bathroom with toilet and shower, and in the bow (front end) there's a small hold for our stores. Most stores were loaded at Port Adelaide, but today we took on my gear and there's still a tonne of chum to come. Yes, chum, or "burley" as they like to call it round here.

By the way, chum is nothing to do with a chum meaning a "pal" or "buddy". It's a nose-wilting, snot-curdling mix of fish guts, blood, fish oil, fish

heads and bits of dead horse. The idea is that great white sharks sniff the chum in the water and come to take a look. Well, it might work with sharks but it doesn't exactly pull in the humans. You'd better believe me, this stuff smells REALLY ROTTEN!

"How bad?" I hear you ask...

Well, each time we picked up a box we held our breath and made faces. The people watching us from the quay, (including Gerald, who's far too important for this humble job) began to edge away with hankies over their noses.

Nathan and I stood on the deck as Katie and Andy handed us down yellow boxes of chum. Note the words "handed down". The *Natalie* was below the level of the quay. Suddenly the lid fell off a box and half the chum sploshed down … all over my head! Everyone roared with laughter, except me.

The taste of that stuff was … well, let's just say I won't be eating fish soup again in a hurry.

There I stood with a fish stuck in my mouth and fish slime dribbling out of my ears. I looked like the victim of a high-speed lawn-mower crash. So this is what it feels like to be shark bait! I thought miserably.

SUN, SEALS AND SEASICKNESS

April 19

This morning the tide was right and the forecast was good and we were ready to set sail. Our first port of call was the Neptune Islands, home of fur seals, sea lions and, if we could find them, great white sharks.

I had tucked into one of Mrs Mallory's huge breakfasts and, laden to the gunwales (as we mariners say), I staggered to the quay. Despite the forecast, the day was blowy with a dirty grey sky. My heart sank as I imagined a bouncy voyage. I *always* get seasick. I can't even go on a boating lake without a bottle of seasickness pills and a large brown-paper bag.

My stomach trembled in terror – but it was too late. I should have thought about that when I answered the advert or scoffed that second helping of bacon, sausage and eggs.

Once we were all aboard, Nathan cast off our moorings and jumped on to the deck. A moment later the ship's engine coughed and spluttered into life. At last we were on our way!

A few minutes later, Port Lincoln was shrinking into the distance and the *Natalie* began to roll. Sickened by the whiff of rotten fish and diesel fuel, I shared my breakfast with the fish.

Gerald was sitting on a deckchair reading a book. He gave me the pitying look that seasoned mariners give to seasick landlubbers. "Try sucking a jelly baby, Sebastian. It works for me…" He offered me a sickly looking jelly baby. It was green.

"I'm Seb!" I groaned. I *hate* being called Sebastian.

"Funny how it affects people," Gerald said. "I've never had a twinge. I love the sea!"

I bent over the rail and unloaded that second helping.

Afterwards, somewhere around Hopkins Island, I felt better. The sun beamed from the clouds and the sea was blue and lively and dotted with foamy waves. Dolphins darted through the clear water around the ship. It was lovely beyond words.

LEAPING DOLPHINS

SEB'S SHARK NOTES
DOLPHINS AND SHARKS

1. Bottlenose dolphins often live in the same waters as sharks and hunt the same fish.

2. Great whites sometimes eat dolphins. If you're in the water with dolphins and they suddenly leave, it might be that a great white has scared them away.

3. There are stories of dolphins shielding humans from sharks or ganging up on a shark and killing it.

The only problem was the cold, wet sea breeze. Soon I was shivering in my T-shirt.

"This'll blow away the cobwebs, Seb!" said Andy, cheerfully taking a deep breath of sea air. "Oh, don't tell me you're cold?"

"I am c-cold," I said through chattering teeth, before going in search of my thermal underwear, scarf and woolly hat.

Nine hours later and 45 km from Port Lincoln, North Neptune Island appeared at last. As we drew closer, I could see the island was surrounded by low cliffs and fingers of rock which stuck up from the blue water.

Tomorrow we're going to land. The Professor wants to look for seals or sea lions with wounds from a great white attack.

April 20

This morning I scrambled into the small boat with the three scientists and we set off for the island. Katie and I were wearing wet suits and clutching our scuba gear because we were hoping to dive with the local seals and sea lions.

I felt excited at the thought of seeing seals but worried about meeting a shark. Mind you, the

Professor said that sharks are so rare, there was little chance of bumping into one during a quick dive, especially as we hadn't put any chum in the water. As we drew near the shore I looked for seals, but I couldn't see any. Where were they hiding?

Andy pointed them out. On the seashore, just behind the line of foam, was a plump fur seal. It looked like a long furry boulder.

Looking a bit harder, I made out more fur seals lazing peacefully on the rocks. They had dark round eyes, black doggy noses, and wide flippers. Their bodies sparkled with watery drops.

One of the seals made three clumsy belly-flopping splat-downs on the rocks, then splashed into the waves. Its shiny head showed briefly above the water, then it ducked down and was gone.

SEB'S SHARK NOTES
SEALS

1. The seals and sea lions are the main reason why great whites live in a certain area.
2. Sharks love the blubbery seal flesh because it's rich in fat and energy.
3. Sharks mostly catch old, sick or weak seals, who can't escape fast enough, but in South Africa, they like to eat seal babies.

Some of the baby seals were huddled together on another part of the beach – they do this when their mums are hunting. Quietly, I slowly crept over the slippery seaweed to sneak a few photos.

AAH! A BABY SEAL

A moment later, I slithered on the seaweed and fell flat on my face. As I picked myself up, I saw the seal babies were staring at a large piece of weed on my head. The furry seal babies are completely helpless, and it's sad to think that if their mums are caught by a great white, they will starve.

WEEDY SEB

Katie and I heaved our scuba gear from the boat and began to "kit up" (that's diver-speak for putting on equipment) and now I felt full of excitement, like a fizzy drink about to go pop. It took us several minutes to strap on our life jackets, watches, air tanks, regulators, fins, and masks. First I spat inside the mask and dipped it in the sea – an old diver's trick (the spit somehow stops the mask from fogging). Then we went over the hand signals divers use underwater and helped each other with our pre-dive checks. Life jacket … regulator … air tank. Tick, tick, tick – they were all OK.

At last, fully strapped up and kitted out like a pair of high-tech frogs, we shuffled backwards into the hissing, whooshing, thundering waves. At once my wet suit lived up to its name, and leaked water. It was so cold I wanted to shout OUCHITSOCOLD! But I didn't because Katie was watching me. Just then a large wave knocked me off my feet and I fell over onto my backside. Katie was laughing as she pulled me to my feet. After that I didn't notice the cold.

OUCH!

We shuffled back a few steps until we caught a wave. Then, breathing the air from our tanks, we dived down into the weird watery world. Underwater, everything is distorted – far things look near and near things blur.

As I dived I felt the usual earache caused by rising water pressure. I pinched my nose and blew down it until, with tiny pops, the tubes between my ears and mouth opened and the ache faded. I breathed out a grumble of bubbles from my mouthpiece and sucked in a hiss of air from the regulator. The only other sound was the muffled roar of the waves. I felt great.

The water was misty near the bottom and Katie and I found ourselves exploring an underwater field of green weed. Here and there sea lions were hiding, but they seemed happy to show off. One glided around me as if to say "hello". It was magic!

SHOW-OFF SEA LIONS

All too soon Katie gave me a thumbs-up sign, meaning that the dive was over. I rolled in the water and glimpsed the daylight rippling above me. Then I darted upwards until I broke the surface in a mass of bubbles.

"WOW!" gasped Katie. "Those sea lions were so cute!"

Before I could answer, a big salty wave splashed into my face and all I could say was "BURBLE-BURBLE-BLUBB!"

Nathan and the Professor had picked their way around every cove and stony beach on the island without finding a single scarred seal. But they did see a dead sea lion with terrible wounds – perhaps a shark victim had crawled on to the beach to die?

I shivered as the chilly breeze blew through my wet suit, but I don't think it was the cold. I looked back at the sea and decided not to risk another dive that day.

April 21

And so to work. We've started chucking chum into the sea to lure the sharks to us. Recently, several great whites have been spotted near the island and the scientists want to find out if any are lurking nearby.

A BEGINNER'S GUIDE TO CHUMMING

1. Sit on diving platform next to box of chum.
2. Dip rusty old pan into stinking blood and fish guts.
3. Lift out dripping pan with foamy scum on top.
4. Tip the slimy stinking stuff into the sea.

Got that? Congratulations – you're a fully-trained chummer!

I easily got the hang of steps one and two. Step three proved a little trickier, and soon there was enough blood to supply a fish blood bank sloshing between my bare toes (I was glad I'd taken Andy's advice and taken off my shoes and socks).

The platform is just a few centimetres above the sea and I kept looking at the water and imagining that a great white was about to leap from the waves and snap me up. Andy says he's never heard of one doing that, but Gerald added cheerfully that you can never be totally sure what a great white will do.

Luckily any hungry great whites had plenty of other food. There were enough chunks of greasy gristly horse meat and smelly tuna trailing on lines for a shark's banquet. Each bait was marked by a  balloon bobbing in the water. If the balloon disappeared it meant that a great white had grabbed the meat dangling beneath.

But so far – nothing. The only fish I've seen are small silvery ones called tommy roughs. Andy says they're like salmon and they always come for a nibble of chum.

As you can imagine, chumming gets boring after the first ten seconds. It's more boring than counting potatoes and almost as boring as listening to Gerald boasting about how he met the Prime Minister. At the end of my shift I felt tired, grumpy and smelly, but Gerald was still droning on and on *and on*…

Several hours later

DISASTER! This morning I forgot to put on my sun block and the sun's been shining most of today. It's easy to get sunburnt at sea because extra sunlight reflects from the water and the cool breeze stops you from noticing the sun's heat. Right now I'm glowing like a radioactive lobster under a sun lamp.

April 26

Two days ago we went back to Port Lincoln to pick up vital stores like water and fuel, and anything we'd run out of such as toilet paper, chum, after-sun lotion and jelly babies… (We'll be going back every week, but I won't mention these trips unless something really interesting happens on them.)

Now we're back at the Neptune Islands, but so far the number of sharks we've seen is precisely *zilch*!

Unfortunately I'm sharing a cabin with Gerald (who takes up 75 per cent of it). His socks stink like a stale cheese factory with a broken ventilator and he snores like a hippo with a serious gut condition.

Nathan and Andy share, and Katie's got her own cabin. They all seem very happy and cheerful and full of jokes. I can't complain because I don't want to sound like a "miserable moaning-minnie" as they say out here. Who would want to swap cabins with me anyway?

Life on board the *Natalie* is as laid-back as a flat tyre. But there's a constant buzz of excitement running through the ship like an electric current. When will we see a shark? What will it do? What will *we* do?

I spend hours reading, avoiding Gerald, writing, scanning the waves for sharks and avoiding Gerald some more. Gerald sits in a chair in his floppy hat, reading scientific articles, munching jelly babies and grumbling about the lack of sharks. Nathan and Katie write about their own shark projects, and Andy looks for things to mend.

A TYPICAL DAY AT SEA

6 am. Wake up, dress, wait ages for Gerald to come out of bathroom.

6.45 am. Breakfast: cereal and long-life milk and long-life orange juice.

7.30 am till lunchtime. Nothing much unless you're on chum duty.*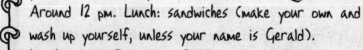

Around 12 pm. Lunch: sandwiches (make your own and wash up yourself, unless your name is Gerald).

Lunchtime to 7 pm. See 7.30 am to lunchtime.

7 pm till suppertime. Supper is always something in a tin heated on a tiny camping stove in the kitchen. (We take it in turns to be cook and washer-upper.)

8 pm to 10 pm. Chill-
out time. In other words
chatting or playing cards
or listening to the radio.
(Some nights Nathan plays
his guitar and Andy plays
his mouth organ, and believe
me, that's better than
a lecture from Professor
Hippo-snore.)
* We all take it in turns to chuck chum for four hours,
but nobody works 4 am to 8 am. Even Gerald grumpily
does his bit, but sometimes he gets so wrapped up in his
book, he forgets what he's doing.

One thing I've learnt this week is how little we
know about great whites. Our ignorance is as wide
as the great Southern Ocean...

SEB'S SHARK NOTES
GREAT WHITE MYSTERIES

It's hard to study great whites. For one thing,
they've got the whole ocean to hide in and
they don't turn up to order. (Don't we just
know it!) Here are just a few questions
scientists want to find the answers to...

1. Why great whites sometimes swim hundreds of kilometres. For example, one once swam 1,850 km from New York to the Cape Verde Islands off West Africa.

2. How many great whites there are.

3. Why the males and females sometimes live apart.

4. Where they go at different times of year.

HA! HA! IT'S A MYSTERY!

April 30

Without even a sniff of a shark, the week has dragged on forever like a rainy Sunday afternoon. The only thrill came yesterday when we drew lots to decide the order we would go down in the shark cage. I was stunned when my name was the first out of Andy's cap. Gerald wasn't too pleased. He sighed and shook his head and went quiet. That evening when I was lying on my bunk, he told me why.

"Look, Sebastian," he began, "we're here doing important research. So far we haven't seen any sharks and it looks like we won't see too many. Couldn't you give up your place in the cage?"

My mind raced. I sat up and banged my head on the roof. I wasn't looking forward to swimming with sharks but I knew I'd come a long way to do it.

"I c-c-can't!" I said as I rubbed my head.

"But, Sebastian," said the Professor, "we need to be in that cage to do our job. One can't get that sort of data from the surface."

Maybe I'd have given up my place if he'd been nicer, but as things stood I wouldn't budge. There was an awkward silence. Then I had an idea. "Maybe I can help," I offered. "Tell me what I can do – take pictures, make notes, or whatever – and I'll do it."

Gerald sat down heavily on the lower bunk. I heard him sigh and then say, "Well, I suppose so. Though it's not ideal, of course."

Gerald has given me a check list of things to look for when I'm diving and I've copied it onto a waterproof pad to take down with me.

SHARK CHECK LIST

Is the shark MALE or FEMALE?
Does the shark have a tag? YES/NO
If YES, what colours?
How long do you think the shark is?
Does it have any unusual markings? YES/NO
If YES – describe them...

Are any of the fins torn or ragged? (Note: these could be the result of bites from other sharks.)
Are any wounds still healing?
Is there any damage caused by humans – for example fishing hooks, bullet holes, etc.?

Last night I dreamt a shark shot me with a gun and I turned into a giant radioactive jelly baby!

May 2

This morning we got bored of feeding tommy roughs on gooey rotten fishy titbits and decided to head for Dangerous Reef.

The reef isn't much to look at. Imagine a few piles of rocks that a tired tortoise could toddle across in a minute with a small shark-viewing platform for tourists. Well, that's it. If it wasn't for the sharks no one would ever go there.

We anchored a few hundred metres offshore and, peering through my binoculars, I spotted two velvet-coated sea lions dozing lazily in the sunshine. The air was alive with scores of seabirds, mostly gulls but some cormorants, all wheeling and flapping and screeching in the gusty wind.

One hour later

I've been watching the cormorants dive for fish – sometimes they catch one, sometimes they don't. Afterwards they rest on the rocks and spread their wings to dry.

Hold on! Katie's just spotted a shark!

"Shark! Shark!" she's yelling.

Everyone's running up to look. My heart's heaving itself up to my mouth. It's the moment I've been dreading, hoping for, having nightmares about. I'll write more when I can…

THE STORY OF SNOW WHITE

Later that afternoon

I've got to write this while everything's still fresh in my mind – every stunning, spine-tingling second – so you can imagine it just the way I saw it.

It took 20 minutes to lower the cage into the sea with a creak and a dull splash. Sharks can hear a cage being dropped three km away, for them it must sound like the cheerful clang of a dinner bell.

As I waited nervously to climb into the cage I was thinking that on a scale of stupid things to do, this rated 11 and a half out of ten. It's worse

than whizzing across the Grand Canyon on top of a giant firework and almost as bad as jumping into a tank of piranhas yelling:

ANYONE FANCY LUNCH?

I wriggled into my diving suit and BCD and picked up my mask with shaking hands. I tried to spit on the inside but my mouth had dried up. The waiting was the worst bit. What would I do? Would I faint? Would I wet myself in my wet suit? Why am I here? I thought, miserably picking up my waterproof pad and pen.

"Try to fill in the check list," said the Professor.

"You can do it, Seb!" said Nathan and Katie.

I wanted to be back at nice safe cosy Greenville School teaching nice kids how to write nice little stories about kittens and flowers and rabbits. But I knew that was impossible.

"I CAN do it! I CAN do it!" I repeated to myself.

As I lowered my body into the cage, I thought my

heart would explode. I glanced nervously at the big black shark's fin just ten metres away. As the murky green waves swallowed me, I felt the cold water leak into my diving suit. Then Andy dropped the cage lid with a loud clang.

I've never felt so alone…

With one hand I gripped the bars like a prisoner. My knuckles were white – either from cold or fear. I looked up at the surface and wondered if I'd make it back in one piece. I was panting so fast that the bubbles were gushing from my mouthpiece. I knew the shark could sense the electic current of fear in my thudding heart. I could just imagine it thinking, *Mmm-mmm-mmm – it's a tasty teacher! It's a shame he's a bit skinny!* I've never, ever felt so scared. It must be like this when you jump from a plane and wait for the parachute to open – *and wonder if it will*. Time had stopped dead in the misty water.

I gazed around wildly, wondering where the shark was – trying to guess where it would strike. But I could see … nothing! Nothing except a few silvery tommy roughs darting around the bait that hung from the ship. And then I saw something moving below me. It was HUGE … and it was ALIVE!

Lazily, slowly, it drifted up from the murky depths. The hairs stood up on the back of my neck. Now IT was up close. IT was swimming past me. I saw the black pits on its snout and the scars on its head. Its face looked grumpy and fierce and there was no expression in its dead, dark eyes. Its mouth was pink and its teeth looked like a suitcase full of knives. Behind the huge head were the gills, like tiger stripes, rippling slightly as the shark glided idly past.

I shrank back into the corner of the cage, picked up the pen and tried to answer the questions. Then I turned and watched the shark with an awe-struck gaze.

SNOW WHITE UP CLOSE AND DANGEROUS

As the shark circled, the underwater light caught its sides and made them gleam silver, and misty sunbeams shone around the depths like underwater searchlights. It was so beautiful I forgot I was supposed to be scared. Instead, I remembered that if a shark moves slowly, it's not going to attack you.

As the shark passed, I made out a white plastic tag and three pale splotches on its dorsal fin. Something told me that this was my shark, the shark I was going to write about in my diary. But the shark didn't know. It nosed past me, no more than three metres away – acting as if I wasn't there.

The shark made three more passes before it turned and faded into the blue haze of the sea. But I didn't want to leave in case it returned and I waited another 20 minutes as the cold chilled my body and made me shiver and shudder all over. At last I tugged the message line to be let up.

Willing hands pulled me into the air. Everyone crowded around me, shaking my hand and slapping me on the back and asking me how I felt.

I sucked in big grateful gasps of delicious cold air. Then I couldn't stop talking. "It was beautiful, unbelievable!" I raved. "I can't believe it! It was incredible, awesome, I've never seen anything like it, I've just got to go back in the water..." And I went on like that for some time...

But afterwards in the shower when I was washing my diving gear in fresh water to protect it from sea-salt damage, I started shaking like a shivering jellyfish. And I just couldn't stop.

WOBBLE
WOBBLE

I'm still as highly strung as a guitar string. Maybe jotting down a few notes will calm me down…

SEB'S SHARK NOTES
SWIMMING SHARKS

1. My shark's leisurely speed was typical. Great whites cruise at a relaxing 3.5 km per hour, but they can power up to 25 km per hour when chasing a seal.

2. A swimming shark shakes its head from side to side. This sends waves of movement rippling down its body. The tail also swings to power the shark through the water.

3. Pectoral fins work like aircraft wings, lifting the shark as the water flows over them.

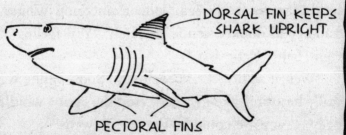

DORSAL FIN KEEPS SHARK UPRIGHT

PECTORAL FINS

4. Although sharks are great swimmers they can't swim backwards and they can't stop once they're moving.

May 3

This morning I felt a bit more relaxed and we gathered in the main cabin to look at the notes I'd made on the waterproof pad.

"Well, she's a female," began Gerald.

"That's right," I broke in. "She had no claspers."

"I reckon this one's been sighted a few times around Dangerous Reef," said Andy stroking his beard.

"Hmm," said Gerald. "The marking and scars are all pretty distinctive, but the white dorsal tag should be enough." He looked up the records of a shark with a white tag. "Her serial number is 331," he announced.

"That's a bit boring!" I protested.

Gerald sighed. "It's all we scientists need," he said.

"No one's ever given her a name," said Andy.

I thought for a bit and a light bulb flickered in my head. "I've got it!" I cried. "How about Snow White?"

They all looked at me strangely. "You feeling all right, Seb?" Katie asked.

"Well, it all fits!" I said excitedly. "Snow White was really beautiful, like my shark. And she's got a whitish belly ... and we could be the seven dwarfs!"

"There's only five of us," said Andy with a rare smile.

"Details, details!" I shrugged, and that was that.

Now for the tricky bit. How am I supposed to write a diary about a fish we know next to nothing about? A creature that turns up without warning and vanishes like a publicity-shy ghost!

Well, I've written a story to fill in the gaps, and here it is… Are you sitting comfortably? OK, I'll begin…

The story of Snow White –
inspired by a well-known fairy tale
(The numbers refer to the notes over the page)

Once upon a time a mother shark had lots of babies, or pups as they're called (1). The babies lived inside their mum, feeding on spare eggs that hadn't hatched into baby sharks.

After a year the mother shark gave birth to the babies, each one about 120 cm long (2). The most beautiful of them all was a pup called Snow White. But now Snow White and the other pups had to make their own way in the world because their wicked mum swam away and left them (3). Soon Snow White's brothers and sisters also went their separate ways.

Snow White was all by herself. She felt lonely and frightened. She had no family or friends to look after her, and she knew she would have to find her own supper. So she set off to catch small fish, crabs or shrimps with her small pointy teeth. Sometimes, she hid in terror from big fierce-looking sharks that looked as if they wanted to eat her for breakfast.

For five long years, Snow White looked after herself, and with each passing year she grew bigger and stronger (4). One day she saw a seal and thought that she would love to eat such a plump tasty-looking creature. Then she began to grow wider teeth that were strong enough to bite a seal. Soon she found out where the seals lived.

All day and all night long, Snow White would swim around the reef in search of seals or large fish to eat. One day she came across the strangest object she had ever seen. It looked like a dead whale with food dangling from it. Snow White decided to visit the whale to feed (5). And that, readers, is the story so far ...

May 4

This evening, after supper, I told the others my story.

"That's really neat!" laughed Katie. "You could have a magic mirror in it too. It might say something like:

MIRROR, MIRROR IN THE WATER, WHO'S GOING TO FIND A SEAL TO SLAUGHTER?

"Yeah," agreed Nathan with a slow nod. "It sounds kinda mystical!"

"The story makes sense," said Andy, scratching a lost toast crumb from his beard.

Gerald nodded slowly. "It matches the known data, so I suppose it's scientific enough."

I suddenly realized that Gerald was actually agreeing with me.

"The problem is Snow White's size," said Andy. "We've got Seb's estimate, but I think I know a way to find out exactly how long a shark is."

"Really?" exclaimed Gerald leaning forward. "It would certainly aid our research if we had some accurate measurements."

Andy explained his plan and I made some notes…

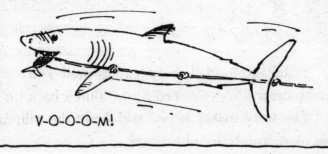

HOW TO MEASURE A SHARK

1. Knot a strong line at one-metre intervals.
2. Secure one end to the ship and tie a hunk of horse-meat bait to the other end.
3. Throw the bait to the shark and when it swims away with the meat, count the knots as the line stretches out along its body.

V-O-O-O-M!

We were so impressed we decided to try it out on the next shark we came across.

Now all we need is a shark…

May 6

"You'd better let the line go if you see a shark," Andy was saying. "If a shark grabs the bait, the line will pull your fingers off or drag you into the sea!"

I gulped. I was at the side of the ship holding the line and Andy was showing me how to feed a shark so we could measure it.

And – can you believe it? – at that very moment I spotted a shark's fin circling the ship. The fin had three splotches – Snow White was back.

"THROW THE BAIT OUT!" roared Andy.

My heart leapt with fright. I gripped the line in my sweaty hand and hurled it with all my strength, almost hurling myself overboard…

"It's too far out!" yelled Andy. "Pull it back in!"

I hauled the now-heavy line out of the still, dark water. At any moment I imagined a vicious yank and my fingers whizzing off like flying bananas, followed by the rest of me. But nothing happened.

"OK," said Andy, "now drop the line."

I dropped it like a scalding potato. A moment later the line jumped – the shark had the bait! The line whipped across the deck and I leapt out of its way. Andy leant forward, counting the knots. "One, two, *three metres!*" he called triumphantly.

WOW! Andy's plan had worked!

Three hours later

I'm writing this in the small boat with Nathan and Andy. We're chasing Snow White! Andy has managed to stick a small sound transmitter that goes PING! every minute into Snow White's back. It's part of the scientists' plan to find out if great whites stay in one place or move from island to island.

Nathan's wearing earphones and dipping a hydrophone into the water trying to pick up the direction of the sound. Andy's yelling into his walkie-talkie to Katie and Gerald, who are on the *Natalie* – and they're plotting the shark's course on a map.

THE CHASE!

The boat is my whole world. All I can hear is the growling engine, all I can smell is the whiff of fuel, and all I can feel is the spray splashing in my face.

The sea is getting rougher. I've been sick three times. I didn't know a body could contain so much vomit. Volunteering to come was one bad move.

One hour later

I'm on look-out duty for Snow White's fin. I'm gazing at the waves as our boat crashes up and down like a roller-coaster ride. It's all right for Nathan and Andy – they love it! They laugh at every stomach-lurching heave and every stomach-heaving lurch.

I shouldn't talk about heaving… Oh, er, now I'm going to throw up again…

A few hours later

When I was feeling a bit better, I took a turn listening to the shark's pings. Then I saw a couple of dolphins leaping from the water beside us and splashing back in graceful dives.

I listened for the signal from Snow White. Suddenly there was an ear-splitting screech – it was as if I had my ear up close to a giant dragging his fingernails down a blackboard. I dropped the mike in the water and tore off my headphones. "AAAGGGGGGGHWHATWASTHAT?!" I screamed.

Andy put the headphones near his ear and laughed. "Dolphin sounds – I reckon they're playing tricks on you."

I rubbed my ears, checking for any leaking blood and brains.

AAAAAGGGH!

HEH! HEH!

We followed Snow White for eight hours in the dark until we lost the signal somewhere to the southwest of Dangerous Reef.

In that time she had led us in two huge loops around the reef.

"I guess Snow White is looking for seals," said Nathan. "She probably stays near the reef all the time."

When we returned to the *Natalie* I felt sick and tired. I was as cold as a frozen pizza. I pictured Snow White swimming off in the dark sea and wondered what thoughts were going through her brain – do great whites even *think* the same way as us?

Then, with my questions unanswered, I lay down on my bunk and closed my eyes…

May 10

This morning when I woke up, the first thing I felt was the *Natalie* shifting uneasily in the water. At breakfast Andy said the weather forecast was bad, but not bad enough to head back to port. Outside, the gusty wind was making the flag flap madly on its twanging line.

Even a landlubber like me could see a storm was brewing. I knew things were going to be rough…

STORMS AND SHARK GUTS

May 10

I was right about the storm. By noon the sky was darkened by thick heavy clouds the colour of pencil lead. I watched lightning flickering across the horizon followed by peals of thunder. Then it started to rain, with a swishing sound over the rising sea.

The waves went from choppy to tippy and from tippy to bet-you-can't-stand-upright, and every time the sea slapped the sides of the *Natalie*, the ship bucked and shuddered. Soon the wind was stirring the

HELP!

sea like a giant's jacuzzi and shooting spray and rain over the ship with a loud whoosh.

Two hundred years ago an English admiral, Francis Beaufort, invented a scale for measuring storms using levels of force. Well, now I've come up with a scale of my own:

SEB'S STORM SCALE

Force 1 - Nice and calm - just the way I like it!

Force 2 - A breeze, but nothing to worry about.

Force 5 - Getting windy, ship starts tipping.

Force 7 - Too stormy to launch cage. Seb groans in bed.

Force 9 - Time to go home. Seb wants to die.

Force 11 - Really stormy. Seb doesn't care if we all drown. In fact he'll be happy to drown as long as it ends his suffering.

May 11

Last night I reckon it was about Force 6. It was my turn to cook and I was bravely having a go. Er – hold on, this isn't a nice story. If you have a delicate stomach you'd better not read it. OK, read on if you *must*, but don't say I didn't warn you!

As the kitchen tipped this way and that, first I saved the beans from falling on the floor and then I saved the saucepans from clattering on my head. I opened the beans and heated them, all the time swaying from side to side, grimly gripping the saucepan. It was the smell of food that made me queasy.

My face went cold and clammy and turned the colour of mushy peas. I felt the familiar faint feeling, the awful churning in my stomach, and then nature took its course — like a drain unblocking. AWMYGAWD! Schalap, globbb, splatter — straight into the saucepan!

Moments later, in walked Andy. "Mmmmm!" he said, sniffing the saucepan. "Looks like bean stew with maybe a hint of parsnip…"

Then the others emerged from the cabins also sniffing the air.

"Something smells nice!" said Katie.

Now, I bet you think I served it up to them, but Seb Walters is far too honest for that! Gritting my teeth I staggered outside onto the heaving deck. Spray stung my face and I slipped on the wet surface. I grabbed the rail and then, dragging myself upright, hurled the smelly sick over the side. The wind blew it straight back into my face. Defeated, I skidded back into the cabin, forced the door shut and stood there, drenched, with sick-misted glasses and spray dripping off the end of my nose.

Four pairs of eyes stared at me accusingly as my crew-mates sat around the table with their spoons at the ready.

"That was my supper!" said Gerald accusingly.

"It was a load of vomit," I replied bitterly.

"Oh, Seb," said Katie brightly, "I'm sure it wasn't that bad!"

Well, I'm going to bed now – I don't feel at all well. I'll try to write more later…

Two hours later

I'm dying, but I've got just enough strength to lift my head off the pillow and write my final words. The storm's still blowing hard and Andy says we ought to head back to Port Lincoln after all. So that's where we're going. Will I live that long? I feel terrible!

May 22

We're still tied up at Port Lincoln waiting for the wind to drop, extra stores to be loaded and a few repairs to be done to the ship. Andy's at home, Katie and Nathan have gone to see their families, and Gerald and I are staying at the Balmoral Hotel.

Today Gerald said that some fishermen working from the shore had pulled in a dead great white. He's bought it with a view to cutting it up and studying its insides. "Want to lend a hand?" he asked me. "It'll be good to put a bit of science in that diary of yours."

Well, I thought you might be as interested as me to see a shark's insides, so I agreed.

On the quay lay the big limp body of the great white. It was one and a half times my length. The shark was dead, VERY dead. It was so dead, my nose took one sniff of its putrid pong and wanted to jump off my face and run away and hide.

ONE VERY SMELLY SHARK

"Course, it's a bit whiffy," said Gerald. "But you've got to suffer for science and it's been ages since I cut up a *Carcharodon carcharias* – that's the scientific name for a great white, you know."

A fork-lift truck picked up the heavy body and drove it to a nearby warehouse. Gerald thanked the driver and he left with a cheery, "No worries, mate – rather you than me!" He didn't want to hang about.

"N-now what?" I asked nervously.

"It's gonna get messy!" said Gerald happily, as he sharpened his scalpel. He began to whistle with the jolly air of someone about to unwrap a huge birthday gift.

I gazed uneasily at the shark. The shark gazed back at me and I saw that the flesh around its jaws had turned an off-putting shade of black. Next to it was a tray with a sinister row of knives, scissors, forceps, tweezers, cotton-wool wipes and the mirrors dentists use to peer into your mouth.

We put on pink plastic aprons and latex gloves and Gerald ordered me to pass him some forceps, a dental mirror and a specimen jar. He was plainly after something.

He put his nose close to the shark's jaws and began to tease out a series of small, red-clawed creatures, each one the size of my little finger. I took a picture of them but tried not to look too closely.

"Ah-ha! Copepods!" cried Gerald, sounding like someone who's found a diamond ring in his cornflakes. "They're small, body-  fluid-sucking creatures that live on sharks. I thought I'd find a few between the teeth."

Then Gerald took his biggest knife and sliced open the shark's belly to reveal huge pink muscles that looked like something you might find in a caravan-sized tin of tuna.

"Great white muscles are remarkable," enthused Gerald. "The blood vessels are arranged to warm the muscles with hot blood. If a great white attacks you, its muscles are already warmed up and ready for action – fascinating!"

They were the sort of fish muscles that cats dream about. But all Gerald did was cut them away and lift the rough heavy blankets of skin on either side. With a grunt of triumph, he tugged out a floppy armful of something yellow and unspeakable.

"Give us a hand, Sebastian!" he called.

"By dame's SIBBBB!" I protested, pinching my nose to block the stink. Holding my breath, I grasped the heavy, slippery mass and between us we dumped it into a plastic box.

"That's the liver," said Gerald cheerfully. "Now all we have to do is weigh it. The liver stores oil that the shark used for energy, so we can find out if our shark's been eating well. It can weigh as much as three humans – but luckily this one's only a tiddler by great white standards."

Between us we heaved the box onto a large set of scales on the floor, and Gerald noted the weight.

"Hmm – a good weight for its size," he said admiringly.

"So the shark ate well?" I asked.

"I reckon so," said Gerald with enthusiasm. "I can't wait to examine the stomach!"

I made a face and tried to ignore the ever-so-ripe smell wafting from the shark and from the plastic box. Readers may like to skip this next bit – in fact you have my full permission!

Gerald rummaged around under another out-sized chunk of muscle and flesh. Then he began to pull out a rubbery, slippery-squelchy, purplish-brown thing. At this point I looked away.

"Aha — here's the stomach!" said Gerald's voice from somewhere inside the shark. "Now let's see what Mr Shark's been eating for supper. Hmm — fascinating ... a squid, a small fish, a few mouldy fish heads ... a paint brush and *streuth*, that looks like a small dog!"

The smell was so bad you could use it to tame elephants, halt riots and knock out buffalo. Just one whiff could silence a school full of half-crazed kids.

By now I was breathing out very fast and clutching my nose very tightly. I found myself taking a sudden interest in my watch and, lifting the cuff of my glove, I mumbled, "Goodness is that the time — only six hours to supper. I'd better go and get showered."

As I walked along Tasman Terrace, I noticed passers-by giving me odd stares and sidelong glances. Only then did I remember I was still wearing my pink plastic apron smeared with yellow shark-liver slime. I must have been wafting a scent trail of long-dead mouldy shark stink.

MOULDY PONG!

Later

When we met for supper, Gerald looked freshly scrubbed and unusually pleased with himself. He ordered seafood stir-fry with noodles and a side dish of pickled onions, and then talked  for an hour about shark eyeballs and tapeworms. I, on the other hand, wasn't feeling too hungry.

May 27

On Sunday we sailed from Port Lincoln with a shore breeze and the morning tide. Although it was hidden behind clouds, the sun shone a silvery path across the water and a gentle breeze swished over the bay.

Whenever he goes to sea, Andy undergoes a personality change. On land he's quiet in a gruff, grizzled sort of way, but on board ship he becomes decisive, full of energy – a leader. As soon as we hit open water he starts using salty sea words like "lash" and "belay" and "berth" and reels off orders to the rest of us.

Standing on the upper deck dressed in his parka and old baseball cap with the wet wind blowing in his beard, he looks every inch a mariner. Andy probably counts sheepshank knots instead of sheep when he goes to sleep. On Monday he showed me how to tie knots – but

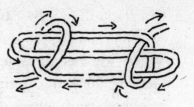

HERE'S A SHEEPSHANK KNOT IF YOU WANT TO TRY IT!

anything harder than shoelaces proved beyond me.

On Tuesday morning, Katie chatted to me whilst I was on chumming duty. We mostly spoke about reef sharks – Katie's pride and joy.

"You can't take them for granted," Katie said, "but they can be gentle. They're big pussy cats really and if I'm relaxed, they're relaxed too."

"Sharks have a nicer side?" I said in a YOU-MUST-BE-KIDDING voice. I tipped a gory stream of chum from the pan and it bloomed like an underwater flower before drifting away in the current. I imagined a distant shark scenting the blood and dreaming of ripping a seal to bits...

"Sure they have a nicer side," replied Katie. "They're so sensitive – when I touch them they just drop down in the water and lean their heads on my lap. They're such sweeties – they *love* being stroked!"

"But they're *dangerous*!" I protested.

"Well, yeah," admitted Katie. "You need to look out for the threat display – if you see a shark arch its back and drop its pectoral fins then it's really angry and it's time you weren't there."

BEWARE OF THIS!

Threat display – hmm – I'll have to remember that…

Two hours later

Katie's interested in how sharks see the world. Here are some of her most fascinating facts.

SEB'S SHARK NOTES
SHARK SENSES

If a shark were a machine you'd call it "A MACHINE FOR FINDING AND KILLING FOOD". The finding part of the job is done by the shark's high-tech sensors:

1. Nose – sharks smell substances in the water that flows into their nostrils. Sharks are after blood – and they're very good at finding it. A shark can sense one drop of mashed-up fish oil in a swimming pool of water.

2. Lateral line – all fish, including sharks, have a groove in their sides. It's lined with sensors that pick up movements in the water.

3. Electro-detectors – the pits on a shark's snout are sensors that pick up tiny electrial currents made in your nerves and muscles and they even sense your heart beating.

MMM – I GET A BUZZ OUT OF YOU!

BATTERY

4. Eyes – sharks can see a 15-cm shape through 18 metres of murky water. Inside their eyeballs they have something called a tapetum that helps them see in the dark. This shiny layer reflects light onto the light-sensitive part of the eyeball.

5. Ears – sharks have a tiny ear hole on each side of their head. Inside the head is a hearing system that also picks up information about the shark's direction and position in the water. A shark can hear a wounded fish 800 metres away.

6. Taste – sharks have taste buds in their mouths and gullet.

May 30

This evening, while the sun was setting, we sat on deck and chatted about the research. The scientists are worried because so far we've seen only one shark – does that mean that there are even fewer sharks left than they expected? None of the experts on the *Natalie* has an answer at present.

Gerald is hoping to find a great white as soon as possible. When we were in Port Lincoln he bought a small dead shark and he wants to observe a great white feeding off its prey. (Prey is any animal the sharks hunt.)

"It's not part of our research aims," he explained. "But it would be a useful opportunity to observe a great white feeding off large prey."

So now all we need is a shark to show up for supper. Here are some facts to set the scene:

SEB'S SHARK NOTES
SHARK TEETH AND FEEDING

1. Great whites have 26 upper and 24 lower front teeth. Each tooth is as jagged as a steak knife and sharp enough to cut your hair – or skin.

OPEN WIDE!

2. Shark teeth are made of the same substance as *human bones*. (That's calcium phosphate if you want to impress your teacher!)

3. Shark teeth can break off, but new teeth are always being made on the inner surface of the jaws – in its lifetime a shark can have 30,000 teeth!

4. When it bites, a shark sticks out its upper jaw and flashes its gums in a scary snarl. Mind you, if the shark was lunching on your leg a snarl would be the least of your worries. Each bite takes just ONE SECOND! Each tooth bites with a force of three tonnes per square cm. That's a bit like you balancing a car on each fingertip!

5. Since sharks don't have flat chewing teeth or cheeks, they have to bite food into chunks and gulp them down whole. And, of course, stray bits of flesh do tend to dribble out of the sides of their mouths – not a pretty sight!

NO DRIBBLING AT THE TABLE!

June 3

Today Snow White ate the dead shark.

It was a lovely afternoon with just a few wispy clouds in the sky. The water was crystal clear, and I could see Snow White's grey back gliding just under the surface while Katie was in the cage taking photos. Andy and Nathan heaved the dead shark out of its box and dragged it across the deck using a hook stuck through its snout. There was a heavy splash as they threw the shark's body overboard.

"Come and get it!" yelled Andy.

Snow White rolled and I glimpsed the underside of her white belly. Then I saw her big toothy mouth and her round black eyes as she dashed at ... the cage floats!

I rushed over to the cage with the others and saw Katie. She was desperately trying to keep her balance.

Then Snow White moved away and I could see the dead shark hanging in the water. Why didn't she eat it? Was she *playing* with us?

Again Snow White butted the float. Then she nipped the carcass. Suddenly she charged, with her pectoral fins as stiff as plane wings. She opened her jaws and smashed into the dead shark in a blast of bubbles. Snow White's body curved with the force of her charge. Again and again she tore at the dead shark making it dance and wriggle on its rope.

The dead shark's flesh hung down in ribbons and its guts trailed out like uncooked sausages. Once more Snow White shook the body until the water clouded with bloody mushy bits of shark. I let out my breath in a long slow gasp. I couldn't help thinking that if Snow White could do that to a dead shark she could certainly do it to one of us.

Afterwards, when Snow White had left, Katie emerged from the water looking pale and shaky. "I've got some really incredible pictures!" she said in a small voice, and burst into tears.

The rest of us couldn't think of anything to say. Soon it'll be my turn to go back in the cage. One tiny slip and I could be the next shark-bait. I've nearly run out of fingernails to chew.

DANGEROUS DINNERTIME!

June 7

This morning we sighted a shark we hadn't seen before. He's a big male, and he's rude even by shark standards. He doesn't circle round like Snow White, he just rushes in, grabs the bait and swims off with it in his jaws. I'm calling him Prince Charming because he's so rude!

HOW CHARMING!

Anyway, Prince Charming doesn't have a tag and the scientists wanted to give him one as soon as possible. Once he's tagged it will be easier to recognize him. And if he dies, anyone who finds his body might return the tag with details of where he was found and how big he was. This will help the Professor judge how fast the shark has been growing.

Gerald wrote out Prince Charming's details on a little form. Andy rolled the paper tightly and pushed it into a thin plastic tube tied to a tiny metal barb. Sticking the barb on a pole, he waited for his chance to pin it on the shark's fin. The barb doesn't harm the shark but it does stop the tag from falling out. Each tag tube has a colour so we'll know the shark again. Prince Charming's tag is a rather girlie pink. Oh well, I don't suppose he'll mind!

Andy popped some gum in his mouth and threw out the baited line. "Come on, Prince (chomp, slurp) – it's time for your jab!" he yelled.

Two hours later he was still throwing, and still chewing. The shark had been too quick for him every time, but luckily Prince Charming was still hungry.

"Got you!" yelled Andy at last, pushing the tag firmly into the shark's fin.

We all cheered. It's funny, but just tagging a shark and giving him a name makes him seem more real, even human. He isn't human, though – I'm sure he'd bite my leg off as soon as look at me!

June 10

This afternoon I found Nathan sitting cross-legged on the deck gazing at a photograph. I peered over his shoulder and saw it was a picture of Nathan himself, standing in shallow water surrounded by man-eating sharks.

"It's my favourite photo, it helps me relax," he said. "I do yoga – it kinda helps me slow down my pulse. The sharks home in on my heartbeat – if they sense I'm not afraid they're less likely to have a go at me."

I knew that next time we saw a shark it would be Nathan's turn in the cage. Nathan closed his eyes in the warm sunshine and a look of blissful happiness crept over his face.

June 15

Nathan got to dive in the cage and so did Andy and so did Gerald. But each of them only dived for a few minutes because the sharks didn't stay too long.

There was just enough time to scribble a few hasty notes and take some pictures.

"Hardly worth getting my feet wet," grumbled Gerald as he heaved himself out of the cage.

I'd been watching from the *Natalie*, and I knew the sharks they'd seen were Snow White and Prince Charming. So now it's my turn again…

June 16

Andy was chewing gum and scanning the sea through binoculars. As soon as he spotted the fin he gave me a quiet nudge and said, "Seb, we've (chomp) got (schlurp) company. You'd better kit up."

HI, GUYS, I'M BACK!

I looked at the shark – it was Snow White. I grabbed my check list. We didn't need more notes on Snow White, but I thought it might be handy if another shark showed up.

I changed quickly. The shark could disappear at any moment and I wanted as long in the cage as possible. I tried to think about what I was doing and ignore my nerves. The odd thing was that I wasn't as scared as the first time. Could it be that Seb Walters was getting more confident with sharks? Could it be he was even getting *braver*?

Once in the water I breathed deeply and slowly, trying to relax as I heard the whistle and hiss of my air supply. When you're in the cage you feel more aware of everything – the finger-tingling thrill of danger, your dry mouth, the whisper of the sea.

The cage swung in the water. I began to feel sick. Oh no, oh NO, OH NO! I thought. I pictured having to scramble out of the cage to chuck up. Slowly my system settled. The water was silent and all I could see were a few tommy roughs nibbling hungrily at one of our baits. But I felt something was going to happen – and soon.

Just then someone on the ship dumped a load of chum in the sea and a current wafted it over my head. Blood, guts and fish goo showered down on me – I waved the murky cloud away and shivered as I pictured my own blood in the water.

Suddenly, through the red haze, I spotted Snow White. She was behind me – very close! I felt as if I was nose to nose with a tiger – but the tiger wasn't interested.

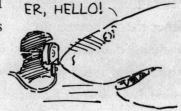

ER, HELLO!

She moved calmly – almost as if I wasn't there. I felt excited – every nerve in my body was stretched to breaking point. I've never felt so awake, so alert. Without thinking, I found myself stretching out my hand to touch Snow White's side as she drifted past. She felt hard and slightly bumpy to my touch. Somehow just touching the shark made her feel more real. Then she was gone…

After what felt like 200 years, Snow White turned, but this time she was keeping her distance. There was another shark close by and this newcomer was bigger than her. It was a male – about five metres, I reckoned. As it approached, the misty light gleamed on its huge grey back. Its jaws widened until I saw the arched gashes of the gills inside its mouth. I found myself thinking that a great white could swallow a child

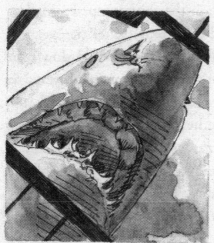

whole. I wasn't a child … but … better not think about it!

Time for a picture, I thought. I looked through my camera viewfinder, waiting for the moment. Waiting for the shark to swerve away from the cage.

But all I could see was a saw-toothed mouth coming straight towards me. I felt hypnotized – I couldn't look away. Still the shark kept coming.

With a crash, the shark hit the cage, forcing its head partly through the bars. I was flung backwards and, falling on the floor-bars, my leg slipped through into open water. Terrified, I tried to pull my leg back through the bars but it seemed to have
jammed! I was just too scared to twist my leg back into the cage. I panicked. I couldn't see either shark – what if one was rushing up to rip off my leg?

Then somehow – don't ask how – my leg was back in the cage. Not a moment too soon! The big shark cruised by less than three metres distant and then turned away, showing its pale belly and the black spots on its sides. It was circling the ship. I looked up and saw that the meat had gone from one of the bait lines. The shark had taken it. Its teeth were so sharp they had sliced through the thick nylon rope as if it wasn't there.

Back it came, closer this time, with its mouth set in a shark snarl, its wing-like fins level. It swung away once more and this time it disappeared into the murky distance.

Shakily, I picked up the notepad from the bottom of the cage where I had dropped it, and scribbled some notes. I tried to remember the scars on the shark's snout, the blotchy outline of its white underside. I couldn't see it now and Snow White had vanished too, leaving me alone.

After maybe ten minutes of waiting I pulled the message line and dragged myself back to the world of air and light.

"Two sharks in one day – you're so lucky!" cried Nathan.

"Well done!" said Gerald, taking my notepad. "It looks like we've found another male shark that hasn't been tagged. It's certainly a result for our research."

I nodded weakly but I didn't have any words left to answer anyone. Instead I sat on the upper deck for a long time gazing blankly at the waves.

Later

I've decided to call the new shark Mr Snapper because that's what he'd probably like to do to me. Everyone laughed when I suggested the name – even

Gerald. I must say, now I'm getting used to him, Gerald's not as bad as I first thought. And he's a mine of shark information just so long as you've got a few hours to spare.

June 23

It's been a shark-less week I'm afraid, readers. But I haven't been bored. It's hard to be really bored at sea – when you've had enough of looking at the waves, the seagulls are fun to watch. Today I've been trying to follow them with my binoculars, swinging the glasses up and down and side to side. I gave myself a stiff neck watching them swoop through the air and floating down to settle on the waves. The seagulls' croaky

WHERE IS IT? –

screeches remind me of the kids at my school!

I've read somewhere that great whites often eat young sea birds, but they don't always like them! So I asked Gerald about what sort of animals great whites like to hunt. That was a mistake – he went on for over an hour in a highly technical fashion about how sharks fit into the life of the sea. Here's a shortened English translation of what he said:

SEB'S SHARK NOTES
FOOD WEBS

The sea is like a nasty school where the medium-sized kids pick on the little kids and the big kids pick on the medium-sized ones – except here "pick on" means EAT. In the sea, most creatures eat creatures a bit smaller than themselves, and great whites are no exception. This diagram is called a "food web" and the arrows show WHO EATS WHO.

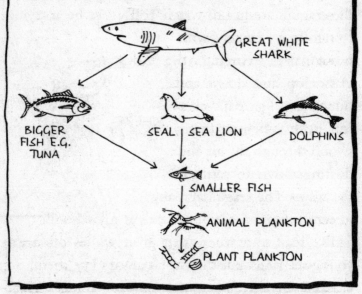

GREAT WHITE SHARK

BIGGER FISH E.G. TUNA

SEAL / SEA LION

DOLPHINS

SMALLER FISH

ANIMAL PLANKTON

PLANT PLANKTON

Of course, real life isn't that neat. Sharks don't tap their victims on the shoulder and say, "Oh excuse me, old man, do you happen to be a dolphin or a tuna fish?" They bite first and ask questions later!

Remember the dead dog Gerald found inside the shark at Port Lincoln? You'll never believe what some sharks eat!

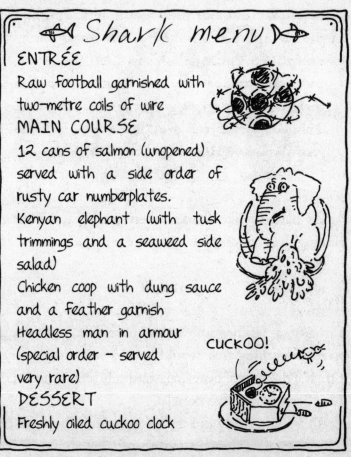

⤜⇇ Shark menu ⇉⤚

ENTRÉE
Raw football garnished with two-metre coils of wire

MAIN COURSE
12 cans of salmon (unopened) served with a side order of rusty car numberplates.
Kenyan elephant (with tusk trimmings and a seaweed side salad)
Chicken coop with dung sauce and a feather garnish
Headless man in armour (special order – served very rare)

DESSERT
Freshly oiled cuckoo clock

CUCKOO!

Yesterday Nathan and I took the small boat to Dangerous Reef. Close up, the elephant-grey rocks looked like lumps of dough crusted by the sea and baked by the sun. Awaiting us was a reception committee of sea lions with big eyes and black flippers. They weren't in the least scared of us – and I got a great picture.

SEA LIONS

It's hard to like sharks when you imagine them sinking their massive jaws into these helpless creatures.

June 30

I'm not a Hollywood action hero but yesterday I tried something that would scare a stuntman's pants off. If I'd known how hair-raisingly crazy my plan was, I wouldn't have done it!

To be fair, Andy did try to warn me. "It could be a bit risky, Seb," he said. But to me that sounded like a challenge. I don't know what's got into me, but I'm definitely more daring. I'd never have dreamt of doing this four months ago!

On the *Natalie*'s aft deck is a lifting arm from

which the cage hangs in the water. The metal arm is three metres long and it has hydraulic cables and levers to make it lift. Anyway, I found out that we have a sling on board that you can tie to the end of the arm to hoist cargo. And that gave me the idea of being lifted up to take an aerial shark photo. It seemed like a good idea at the time. Take it from me, *it wasn't*!

Snow White showed up about 8 am and I stepped into the sling. It's like putting on a giant red plastic nappy that comes up to your armpits.

With a jerk, Andy hoisted me into the air and there I was, dangling two metres above the sea. As the ship heaved and tossed in the water, I swung from side to side. Then I saw Snow White. I could see her black eyes and pointed snout rising above the surface – she was spy hopping. That's what it's called when a shark peers out of the water at you.

SNOW WHITE SPY HOPPING

And then the horrible truth dawned… As the ship dipped in the water, my bare legs were only a few centimetres above the waves! Sharks can leap two metres to grab prey, so I was a sitting duck!

With a sickening sinking feeling, I watched the great dark form of the shark circling below. I could clearly see her powerful head and her waving tail. What would she do? What could *I* do? Slowly, I raised my legs in the air.

Just then I heard cursing from the ship. Andy was signalling frantically. "It's jammed!" he yelled. "*We can't get you down!*"

Chilly spray splashed my skin – I imagined dangling all night like a puppet on a string. Or maybe Snow White would get hungry and decide to snack on my legs… I waited and worried as Andy fussed and fiddled with the lifting controls. At last, when I thought all was lost, I felt a shudder and the arm jerked … *down*! My legs dipped into the water and I let out a cry of horror as I saw Snow White heading my way. A second later I felt something brush against them. But was it a brush? I once read that's how a *bite* can feel! My whole body went cold. I pictured the squirting blood, the horror. *Had I been bitten*?

Frantically I heaved my legs out of the water, swinging backwards in the sling. There was blood all right, but it was only a graze! It was a scrape made by the shark's rough skin as she brushed past me.

Just then the arm lifted with a groan and a rising screech of metal. I was raised up and swung down, bouncing like a human yo-yo. Then I was hurled wildly sideways and tipped headfirst into an open box of slimy fishy chum-goo. I spat out a fish's eyeball and picked myself up. And decided then and there that I'd never mess with the lifting arm again.

SCHPLATT-GLUBBBB!

Later

Luckily my graze isn't too bad. Gerald dabbed it with some iodine (which stung so much it brought tears to my eyes) and strapped on a bandage. I feel just about OK, but I can't help thinking that I've had a lucky escape... And luck doesn't last for ever.

TELLING TALES

July 5

Four shark-less days, but I've got some great stories to share with you. Yesterday we sat on the upper deck, gazing at a wonderful multi-coloured sunset and telling each other shark stories…

"About 100 years ago," began Nathan, "in Port Phillip, Australia, there was a swimming pool for ladies in a fenced-off part of the seaside. One day the ladies complained to the caretaker that a great white shark had been watching them through a gap in the fence."

"Were they scared of being eaten?" asked Katie.

"No, oddly enough, this was 100 years ago and the ladies thought it was rude for anyone to see them in their bathing cozzies, even a shark!"

"Very amusing," said Gerald, "but I've got a scientific story." I braced myself for a long lecture. "A US navy commander named Donald Baldridge," he began, "was fascinated by sharks. He decided to find out if they were attracted by a creature struggling in the water…"

"So he jumped into the sea?" suggested Katie.

"Not exactly. He got a rat and tied its tail to a fishing line and lowered it into a pool of sharks."

THIS IS GOING A BIT TOO FAR!

Katie's mouth made an O shape. "But that's *cruel!*" she gasped.

Gerald shrugged. "The rat was OK," he said. "The sharks were curious and bumped it a couple of times, but they didn't bite it. In fact they preferred eating fish. So the next thing Baldridge did was to dip the rat in mashed-up fish juice…"

Andy stroked his beard thoughtfully. "It's funny," he said, "we humans like to think we're tasty, but to a shark we might taste of old socks and creaky shoe leather. They might well prefer their usual fish or seals. Great whites often take a bite out of a human and spit it out."

YUK!

SEB'S SHARK NOTES
SHARK ATTACKS

1. Three types of sharks are considered the most dangerous: the bull shark, the tiger shark and, of course, the great white.

2. Some scientists think great whites attack humans by *accident*. Many attacks happen in murky water or surf, where the shark can't see the human properly and mistakes them for a seal. Here's a shark's eye view of a seal and a surfer as seen from below.

3. The risk of being attacked by a shark is actually quite low. These figures from the USA may surprise you...

• Four times more people get taken to hospital in New York as a result of vicious hamster attacks than get injured by sharks in the *entire country*.

- **30 times more people get struck by lightning than attacked by sharks.**
- **2,400 times more people get injured by toilets than hurt by sharks.**

We talked for ages as the twilight colours deepened and the light slowly disappeared. Finally, when it was dark, we went to our cabins feeling relaxed and happy.

July 6

Last night's shark stories left me wondering what a great white attack actually *feels* like. This morning I asked Andy if he'd ever been attacked.

He shook his head. "But a mate of mine has…" Andy swallowed the gum he was chewing. "Surfer, name of Matt. About a dozen years ago he was riding the breakers near Port Adelaide. There he was, happily splashing, as innocent as a baby seal. Little did he know, a shark was beneath him, eyeing him up with its cold black eyes. Matt felt a brush on his leg – like seaweed. That's what everyone feels…."

"It can be a bump or a terrible bite," I said. "It all feels the same."

Andy nodded. "Matt looked down and saw the shark looking back at him."

"I bet that gave him a shock!" I said.

"Just a bit!" Andy grinned.

"So what did Matt do?" I asked.

"He kicked. That's what you're supposed to do, but only when you're in the gravest danger. He kicked the shark's nose. He was lucky – if his foot had gone in the shark's mouth, he'd have lost it."

I pictured the scene and shuddered. "What did the shark do?" I asked.

"Well, sometimes they swim off, but this one did what I'd do – it got mad and attacked him. It sank its jaws in a great semi-circle, ripped off a bite and swam away. Matt can't think about it without crying." Andy shook his head and sighed.

"Was he terribly injured?" I asked anxiously.

OH SPIT!

"He wasn't, it was his *surfboard* that got bitten. Matt says it was the best darned board he ever had." Andy laughed. "Didn't stop him, though. He was in the water the next day!"

If a shark attacks and bites you without warning what possible defence is there? Well, it's surprising the weird and wonderful methods people have tried...

SEB'S SHARK NOTES
DEFENCES AGAINST SHARKS

1. Anti-shark weapons (eg bang-stick, spear gun and billy stick): protection rating 5/10. Some scientists carry weapons to fight off a shark – the problem is that if you don't kill the shark it might feel upset and kill you instead.

2. Anti-shark chemicals: protection rating 8/10. Scientists have found that sodium lauryl sulphate, a chemical used in shampoo, drives sharks away. You squirt it down their throats. The shark makes a nasty face and has to gulp lots of water to wash out the terrible taste.

3. Electronic defences: protection rating 8/10. A POD (that's a Protective Oceanic Device if you want to sound like Gerald) produces an electric field that upsets sharks and makes them twitch. But things could turn nasty if your battery goes flat when you're surrounded by hungry sharks.

4. Chain-mail suit: protection rating 7/10. Katie wears one of these to cuddle sharks. Developed in the 1980s, the chain mail protects you, but smaller sharks can bite between the metal links and great whites can crush your body like a cola can. The electric currents in the metal might even make sharks more interested in you.

5. Floating nets: protection rating 9/10.

Today some beaches in South Africa and Australia are shielded by floating nets. Unfortunately sharks often drown in the nets and so do harmless dolphins and turtles.

6. Anti-shark dolphins: protection rating 0/10.

A dolphin named Simo was trained to attack small sharks at Mote Marine Lab, USA, but he got scared and swam away when faced by a bigger shark. Can anyone blame him?

July 10

This week's weather has been dry and cool and windy. It's typical for the time of year.

Andy's often talking about the weather – he listens intently to the morning weather forecast and when I ask him what we're going to get, he says,

"It'll be fine again" or "Nothing we can't handle".

Today I asked him if there was any weather he couldn't handle, and he muttered something about a sou'-westerly force eight, a broken engine and a lee shore.

For you, sitting in your comfy wherever-you-are, the weather isn't exactly white-knuckle, page-turning reading. But for us out here the weather is crucial. I mean it could even kill us, as I learnt in that storm back in May.

Today we've been telling some more shark stories to while away the time.

"Of course," said Gerald in his best you're-in-for-a-lecture voice, "Australia is the only nation on Earth where the Prime Minister got eaten by a shark. In 1967 Harold Holt went for a swim – and never came back."

"Oh come on!" protested Nathan. "No one ever proved it was a shark that got him. It might have been a rip current that swept him away."

Gerald snorted crossly, but fortunately Katie stepped in before an argument started. "I've got a different kind of story," she said. "It may or may not be true. Hundreds of years ago, native Indians who lived by Lake Nicaragua in Central America threw dead bodies to the sharks. The bodies were dressed in fine jewellery, and a European settler found that he could catch the sharks and pick jewels from their stomachs. Then the Indians heard about it…"

"Oh, don't tell me," said Gerald. "They fed him to the sharks…"

"No," said Katie crossly. "That's the point. They killed him and burnt his house down, but they didn't feed him to the sharks. You see, he wasn't good enough for that!"

"I kind of get your drift," said Nathan. "Humans always make out that sharks are the bad guys, but who are the cruel ones in this story?"

"Not the sharks," agreed Katie. "They only did what sharks always do."

As we talked, the first stars brightened in the evening sky. A glow appeared on the horizon, followed by a bright yellow semi-circle. Slowly the moon rose and shone a glittering path across the sea.

Katie turned to me. "What about you, Seb? You've heard our shark stories – I bet you've got a ripper one!"

My brain went blank, but then it clicked into gear.

"Well," I said. "I don't know any stories that *really* happened, but I suppose I could tell you a story that *hasn't* happened yet. The story of Snow White's later life…"

"That's neat," said Katie. "It's kind of like a sequel – the return of Snow White."

I cleared my throat. "One day, about six years after she found the funny dead whale, Snow White was swimming around the reef when she met a handsome prince. Of course, it was love at first sight…"

"Love?" Gerald snorted. "Sharks don't have complex emotional feelings!"

Katie shushed him and I went on with my story.

"Er, sorry, Gerald. I meant to say Snow White came across a big male shark – maybe it was Prince Charming. He nipped her dorsal fin, to get her in the mood, and

OOOH, YOU'RE ᔕOOO ROMANTIC!

they mated. Then he swam off, leaving Snow White with an ugly scar and babies growing inside her."

"That sounds far less romantic," said Katie.

"But more factual," said Gerald approvingly.

"You could have Snow White turning on Prince Charming and eating him," said Katie. "Some great whites do – now that's what I call girl power!"

"A year later," I continued, "Snow White had ten little shark pups and left them just as her mother had left her. Like other sharks and most humans, as Snow White grew older she became bigger round the middle and greyer on top. And that's all I can tell you except she lived a long life – is 30 years about right for a great white?"

They all nodded.

"And so she lived happily ever after."

Gerald shook his head. "I can see you're not a scientist, Sebastian. I wouldn't commit myself to predicting the future in this way. Snow White could easily end up gasping in a fishing net."

"Oh shame!" said Nathan.

I began to chew my remaining fingernail. Of course it's only a story, I thought later, as I lay in my bunk with my fingers in my ears, trying to block out Gerald's explosive snores. But it's going to happen for real one day and it could end happily … or unhappily.

SNAPPING SHARKS AND DEAD, DEAD DUMMIES

July 12

This morning's excitement began when we spotted a seal paddling behind the *Natalie*. It didn't seem at all scared. I watched the seal for about an hour and then Gerald shouted that there was a shark on the way. The seal had sensed it too – it stopped playing and huddled close to the ship, shivering with terror.

We could see the great shadow of the shark in the clear green water. As it drew near, the seal made a dash to escape, but the shark was after it. It was Katie's turn in the cage and she quickly kitted up, pulling her wet suit over her head and stretching the neck until first her sun-bleached hair and then her excited face appeared at the opening.

Meanwhile the rest of us watched open-mouthed as first the seal and then the shark leapt clear of the water with explosive splashes. It's called breaching and it's amazing!

PRINCE CHARMING BREACHING

After 20 minutes of the chase I think the seal must have got away because the shark slowed. By then we'd seen the pink dorsal fin tag and knew that the shark was Prince Charming. We watched to see what he'd do next. He broke the surface, opened his big sharp jaws and began to bite the waves.

"He's gaping," said Gerald.

I nodded. Sharks do this when they're cross and right now Prince Charming looked ready to chew the sea floor.

"What a brave little seal!" gasped Katie as she clambered from the cage.

SEB'S SHARK NOTES
HUNTING

1. None of our experts are too sure how often great white sharks hunt or catch their prey. Gerald says they need about 60 seals or 11 tonnes of meat a year. (According to Nathan that's equal to 97,000 hamburgers.)

YUM! YUM!

2. Great white sharks usually attack from beneath because they can see the outline of their prey, and if the prey's caught on the surface, it can't dive deeper to escape.

3. If there's more than one shark around, the biggest shark gets to hunt and the others back off.

4. A great white shark hits its prey with the force of two cars and enough power to whack a human into the air. At the last minute, its eyeballs roll backwards for protection. The shark often bites once and then circles as the wounded victim bleeds to death.

5. Some seals and sea lions do escape. They're fast swimmers and often dodge the great white or fight back with their teeth and claws, scratching the shark's sensitive snout.

A few minutes later, I was on the diving step. Suddenly I felt like I was sliding on a slippery banana skin. I couldn't stop and a second later I sploshed into the water. All I could see was green sea and bubbles. After a moment I bobbed to the surface and reached out for Andy's hand. Thirty seconds after that, I was dripping on the deck.

Then it hit me. I was lucky to be alive! If there's one thing worse than falling in the sea, it's falling in the sea on top of a hungry great white shark in a bad mood. I'd better watch my step from now on.

July 15

Ever since I first met Andy and he said he wanted to swim with a great white, I've felt that behind that calm smile lurks a genuine wacko crazy. The sort of person who gets a buzz from hanging around seriously savage sharks. Today Andy showed his true colours. As we divers say, he's completely "flippers".

Today he tried to tickle a great white. Yes, you read that right. I said "tickle" – T-I-C-K-L-E – that's the technical term for it.

IT'S NOT THAT KIND OF TICKLING!

We were standing on the deck watching Snow White circle the ship. Andy was telling us that great whites have different "personalities" – some are fiercer than others and some are more scared of us, and so on. Snow White isn't that fierce according to Andy.

"It's a lovely feeling being close to a great white," mused Andy. I must have stared at him too long because he said, "I *mean* it, Seb, I really love it when I tickle them. Have you ever seen it done?"

I shook my head numbly.

"You lean over, and when the great white comes up you just touch the point of its snout and push it away." Andy jumped on to the diving platform. He knelt down and stretched out his hand towards the shark.

I watched this lunatic, speechless with horror. It was then that I knew the truth – Andy Hawkins is madder than a squirrel in a nut farm! But none of us stopped him. Maybe we were too stunned. Or perhaps we just didn't believe our eyes.

The sea was like green glass and I could see the huge shape of Snow White in the water. A moment later her snout broke the surface in a widening circle of ripples, then she dived again. She was coming our way, but Andy didn't move. Again the snout rose. This time I saw her pink mouth. It was the colour of blancmange and ten million times more deadly. Coal black eyes stared blankly at Andy. Gently he pushed the shark's nose and incredibly Snow White let him, rolling her body in the water.

IS THIS MAN FOR REAL?

"It feels good," exclaimed Andy as the shark dropped deeper.

Moments later she was back. Again Andy gently pushed her away. To my utter amazement I realized the shark was playing. She was actually *enjoying* being shoved! As I watched, Andy ran his finger lightly over Snow White's upper lip. His hand was just inches away from the rows of razor teeth that could rip his arm off in a second.

"I do it," said Andy, "because I like it, and the shark does too. Anyone fancy a go?"

My mouth fell open. One by one we made our excuses, even Nathan who feeds sharks by hand and Katie who cuddles them. I don't know what I stammered, but Andy got the message. The sport of shark tickling isn't about to catch on...

July 18

Today we saw and tagged another shark. I'm calling the newcomer Cinderella because it looks like she's had a hard life. She's a five-metre-long female with a ragged dorsal fin. The poor creature had a length of net twisted around her right pectoral fin and a fishing hook stuck in her belly. I don't think Cinders is going to make it to the ball, but there's nothing new about humans harming sharks. Did you know that for every human killed by sharks TWO MILLION sharks die at the hands of humans?

WOE IS ME!

SEB'S SHARK NOTES
SENSELESS SHARK PRODUCTS

1. Before the trade in great white body bits was banned, their jaws were sold to tourists and their teeth were made into jewellery.

2. Up to the 1940s, shark oil was used to make vitamin A pills and to oil machinery.

3. Shark skin was also used to make dagger sheaths. In ancient Japan, angel shark skin was used for sword handles because the rough skin didn't go slippery when soaked with blood.

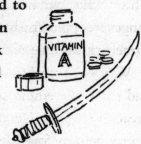

4. Shark's-fin soup is made out of a shark's fin (surprise surprise), but the rest of the shark is chucked away. Only the fin rays go into the soup and they're tasteless, yet people pay lots of money for this cruel mockery of cookery.

Nowadays, in Australia, the USA and South Africa there are laws that protect great white sharks, but their numbers still seem to be going down. We were talking about this over supper and Gerald said that seeing as we've only seen four great whites in three months, it looked like the reports were true.

Everyone nodded unhappily. Well, after finding

out so much about them and after seeing them with my own eyes, I've come to care about sharks in a strange way, so I really, really hope Gerald's wrong (for once).

July 21

This is my last week in Australia. I'd love to stay longer but the expedition is nearly over and the hire-agreement for the *Natalie* is coming to an end.

We've managed to study four great whites, and I've had some incredible, terrifying meetings with these great fish. But Gerald's itching to try one last experiment before we return to Port Lincoln. It's nothing to do with the research, but he's wondering whether scientists are right when they say there's less chance of a shark attacking you on the sea bed. And he's thought up an experiment to find out.

We've dressed a dummy (kindly donated by Chloe's Clothes of Port Lincoln on our last visit) in a diving suit, and we're going to leave it on the sea bed to see if a shark will attack it. They're calling the dummy Seb because it's skinny like me. Let's hope they don't use me by mistake, eh, readers!

SPOT THE DUMMY!

July 22

Tomorrow we're going to try the dummy experiment. You should have seen Gerald's face when I offered to put Seb the dummy on the sea bed.

"*You*? You don't mean it, Sebastian!" he gasped. "It's a risky experiment, you know."

"It's named after me, isn't it?" I said firmly.

The others laughed. "I think Seb's kinda made up his mind," said Nathan.

July 23

If a floating fortune-teller had told me what would happen, would I have gone down with the dummy? I can't say. It's best not to think. But the really amazing thing – and I bet you don't believe me after my nasty brush with Snow White – is that I didn't feel scared about taking on the job!

I felt quite cramped as I was lowered in the cage with the dummy. The cage is only big enough for one person and I was glad the coast was clear of sharks as we gently descended. It felt like I was in an underwater lift. "Going down, basement for dummies, sand and seaweed," I wanted to say.

The sea bed looked like a sunken field, with crabs instead of cow poo. I pushed open the hatch door at the top of the cage and hauled myself out. My weight belt was heavier than usual to help me walk on the sea bed, and I felt clumsy and laden down. I pulled the dummy from the cage, climbed down to the sea floor and set off in the dim turquoise twilight in search of a good site to leave it. My heavy boots sank into the soft sand. It was hard to move faster than a slow, sluggish shuffle.

GRUMBLE, GROAN

Just then a movement caught my eye – I knew at once it was a shark. If it came at me I couldn't even stumble away. I'd never reach the cage in time.

All at once a second shark appeared. Typical! I wait weeks to see a shark and then two come along at the same time! This one was big, maybe five metres long. Some tiny brain cell that wasn't fizzing in panic shouted that it was the dreaded Mr Snapper, the shark I'd seen on my second dive. The one that hit the cage … *the fierce one.*

As I watched, the shark dropped its pectoral fins, arched its back and surged upwards to butt the underside of the ship.

I heard a muffled crash and the surface dissolved into grey bubbles, and then I saw two thin dark legs. Human legs! Someone was in the sea! The shark must have knocked them in. But why wasn't the person swimming? *Could they be dead*?

The figure drifted helplessly away and the shark swam between the human and the ship. Even from below I could hear the crack of the shark's huge tail. I didn't think, I just acted. You must be the judge of how stupid or brave I was. Right then, there was no time to be scared. Somehow I hatched a plan.

Holding my breath, I took the pipe from my air tank and filled the dummy's life jacket. The dummy took off for the surface like a guided missile. I watched it rise, and my heart hammered inside my chest as the shark closed in on the dummy. In a moment the figure was in the shark's jaws, being shaken violently from side to side. That could have been a real human – *that could have been me*!

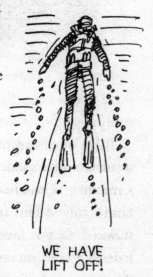

WE HAVE
LIFT OFF!

I flipped open the quick-release clip on my weight belt and kicked towards the surface, hissing out a steady stream of bubbles to avoid bursting my lungs. To my right, I caught sight of the first shark. I saw her dorsal fin, and knew she was Snow White.

Snow White came closer. I saw her black eyes and her dagger-like teeth. I saw the great jagged gash of her mouth and knew she could kill me. But somehow I wasn't scared. She swam closer and closer. But she wasn't coming for me, she was gliding between me and the other shark. It sounds crazy but it was almost as if she was shielding me, protecting me.

BACK OFF!

It all happened in seconds. The next moment my head was above water in the foam and light and air. I reached for the man in the water, cupping back his chin to allow him to breathe. Now I could see who it was… It was Gerald! His eyes were closed in his pale face. His clothes were wet and heavy and his beard and hair were soaking. But he was still alive.

I held him in my arms, pulling him onto his back in the water. The sharks must be closing in. There was no time. No time to be scared – no time to hear the warning shouts and screams from the ship. I kicked my feet in one last desperate push.

HANG IN THERE!

Andy reached out. With a grunt and a heave he dragged Gerald's body onto the diving platform. A moment later Nathan pulled me out of the water.

Suddenly my legs felt weak and wobbly and the others had to help me take off my diving gear. All I could do was sit there, soggy and shivering, in the hazy sunlight.

Later that afternoon

I asked Katie what had happened when I was underwater. She shook her head and brushed a stray hair out of her eyes. "Phew, it was a real close shave!"

she said. "When the shark hit the ship we were all knocked off our feet. Andy said some colourful words and then we saw that Gerald wasn't on the platform. We didn't hear the splash."

"So what did you do?" I asked.

"We rushed to the sides shouting, 'GERALD, WHERE ARE YOU?' He'd knocked himself out on the diving platform as he went in, and by the time we spotted him the shark had cut him off. Just then we saw the dummy and we reckoned it was you. When the shark went for the dummy, I screamed. It was incredibly scary!"

Later that evening

I met Katie and Nathan in the main cabin.

"How is Gerald?" I asked.

"He's fine," said Katie. "He was talking about the experiment – reckons it must mean the sea bed is safer than the surface."

"At least he's healthier than the dummy," added Nathan. "We found it floating in the sea with its right arm and leg missing."

POOR OLD DUMMY!

Just then Gerald appeared at the door. Katie took in his pale, sickly face and said, "Gerald, are you feeling all right? You really ought to be resting."

Gerald swayed and touched the big sticking plaster on his forehead. "Really, I'm right as rain. I just wanted to thank this young man." He gave me a dazed smile and shook my hand weakly. "Thanks, Seb — I reckon you saved my life!"

July 25

At dawn this morning, Andy weighed anchor and steered the *Natalie* towards Port Lincoln. I leant on the rail listening to the throb of the engines and felt the ship pushing through the dark, still water. I was hoping for a last glimpse of Snow White but I never even saw a fin. I stared into the silvery morning mist and apart from the engines all I could hear was the slap of the empty sea. Where was she? That's the trouble with sharks – they're never around when you want them.

RETURN TO DANGEROUS REEF

December 2

I answered the advert for a dare. I wanted to prove to myself and the other teachers that I was brave enough. But this diary hasn't been about me; it's been about the sharks – how they live and how they seem to be dying out. After I went home, I couldn't get Dangerous Reef out of my head. I talked about it and thought about it every day.

But now I am back – this time as a tourist. Earlier today I went out on the *Natalie*. I stood on the deck next to Andy as she chugged through the blue water. I felt grateful the day was so calm. The sea was almost as still as a pond, and I hadn't even thought about being seasick. I was looking for the dark triangle of a shark's fin. A fin with three white splotches.

As I gazed at the sea, I thought about how swimming with sharks has changed me. Now I feel fearless, I'm not afraid of anything. All the kids in my class think I'm a hero and Mr Masham and the others don't tease me any more. And I don't have bad dreams about sharks. I know that sharks are more than the silent killing machines of my nightmares – they're creatures of power and grace.

I've kept in touch with the rest of the team by email and letter.

Katie is back making friends with reef sharks. She says she's not sorry she missed kissing a great white.

Nathan still feeds bull sharks, he says he feels closer to them than ever.

Gerald is teaching at University. He says that nearly dying has made him realize what's important in life — like having friends. And he now calls me Seb.

But what of Snow White? Was she still alive? Despite the ban on shark fishing, great whites are still being caught by accident in fishing nets. No one is sure exactly how many great whites live off South Australia, but their numbers are dropping all the time.

I imagined the reef some time in the future when there are no more great white sharks cruising the murky waters. It might be a risk for ships but it

won't be as DANGEROUS any more. All that would be left is a sad lump of rock without any magic or mystery.

Suddenly I heard a shout. "Look over there — it's a shark!"

Everyone rushed to the side of the ship. People whispered excitedly. Fingers pointed and cameras clicked. A little boy grabbed his mum's arm.

I watched him staring wide-eyed, half sheltering behind his mother. I looked at his face, peeping out and biting his lip, half scared and half amazed.

I stared at the shark's fin through my binoculars ... and then I saw them – three white splotches. "It's Snow White!" I cried out, unable to believe my eyes.

Andy and I shook hands.

"I knew she'd want to see you!" he grinned.

"That means she's all right," I said happily.

For half an hour we watched Snow White circle the *Natalie*, now and then rising to take the baits that Andy threw to her. Sometimes the little boy would point and yell "there she is!" He wasn't scared any more. Then, quite without warning, Snow White left us. The ocean closed over her with a watery sigh. She had gone back to the world of shadows, leaving only the silence of the sea.